A Blessing in Disguise

WHAT CANCER TAUGHT ME ABOUT LIFE

Richard Kingsley

What Cancer Taught Me About Life
Copyright © 2023 by Richard Kingsley

All rights reserved. No part of this publication may be reproduced, distributed, or transmitted in any form or by any means, including photocopying, recording, or other electronic or mechanical methods, without the prior written permission of the author, except in the case of brief quotations embodied in critical reviews and certain other non-commercial uses permitted by copyright law.

Tellwell Talent
www.tellwell.ca

ISBN
978-0-2288-8945-8 (Paperback)
978-1-7794-1331-4 (eBook)

Table of Contents

Touched 3

Live in Hope 4

My Blessings 5

Self-Worth 6

Memories 7

Looking Back 8

The Pandemic 9

Cruising 12

Western Samoa 15

Hawai'ian Islands 16

Tahiti 20

New Zealand 23

Home 24

Attitude 26

Travel 27

Work 29

Papua New Guinea 33

Flying 36

Healing Work 38

Bee Sting 42

Australia 43

Nature's Plan 45

Full Circle - Life Lessons 47

Acknowledgements 51

First, some ground rules . . .

Do not feel sorry for me, I'm doing fine. The main things I still have to deal with are routine check-ups and some minor aftereffects of the radiation treatment. I always remind myself that there are people who are a lot worse off than me.

To begin with, I'd like to provide a few thoughts to keep in mind while reading this book.

I promise not to use Google, this will all be from my own memories and experiences, with nothing political or religious. Everyone has their own experiences and beliefs. There would be peace if everyone respected everyone else -—we often hear people say, "you want your beliefs to be respected, don't you?" Also, nothing about my personal relationships; suffice it to say I have loved and been loved by some wonderful people in my life.

"I have been a puppet, a pauper, a pirate, a poet, a pawn, and a king." These are words from a great Frank Sinatra song. *Cycles* by Sinatra and *Desiderata* by Les Crane are both inspiring and meaningful songs to me. See what you think.

I've been inspired by many things, mostly the words to songs—they invoke good and loving memories, but also sometimes give you direction—certainly they make you think, as the lyrics were written by some brilliant and beautiful people.

Sometimes you spend all your life trying to please others because you're conditioned that way, reaching out for love!

I saw a film called *The Dove*, which was the true story of Robin Lee Graham sailing around the world solo as a seventeen-year-old. He almost gave up at one point. He was doing it for everyone else . . . and then he said, "I have to finish this trip, I have to finish this trip for myself!" Those simple words have stuck with me all my life. Thank you, Robin!

I had been a lost soul for a long time. I found out why later, at age 33! I'll explain about that later.

TOUCHED

Almost everyone has been touched by cancer. You either know someone who has it, or you have it yourself or have had it. There are blessings in being sick. What do I mean by that? That's what this book is about!

Mum and dad both had dementia. They were both in a nursing home when dad died. Mum was in the TV room. The staff prepared him, and then we took mum to see him. She touched him and said, "I've lost my Reg." By the time we took her back to the TV room she had forgotten the sorrow she had expressed and had no memory of dad's passing—that's one example of a blessing!

LIVE IN HOPE

Almost every person I have met or known who had cancer or an affliction of some kind—possibly because of it—is the most wonderful soul you could ever wish to meet.

Many agree that it was the best thing that had ever happened to them. These people are at peace with what has happened to them, and only see it as an inconvenience.

At the Paralympics, where I was privileged to be an official, I was awed by the extraordinary attitudes, the humour and the humility that these wonderful people expressed. They always challenged themselves.

I refereed an under-sixteen tennis tournament a few years ago, and the loser of the girls' final sat down and cried her eyes out. I got on the microphone and said to everyone, that there isn't a tennis player in the world that hasn't lost a match. Learn from it and adapt—that's what sick people do!

My Blessings

After retirement, my days and weeks were filled with sleep-ins, lots of coffee and not much else. My blessing was that it brought my family closer together, especially my beautiful children, with whom I had lost contact to some extent.

I learned that there is beauty in everyone, wisdom and wonder in the world. Nature is amazing and we need to learn from it. It mostly adapts to its own environment.

What is the essence of life? It's all about relationships, memories and loving and being loved—by all the people in your life and most importantly, yourself!

Life is very precious, not for what you do—your job or profession—but for what you experience in life, the person you have become because of all that has happened to you. The happiness and joy that these experiences gave you, the people you love and have loved, or just being in a particular place that resonates with you, and you don't even know why, all shape you into who you are.

This is where all of your memories come into play. Growing up, my children never got presents, they had experiences. They were given things like a helicopter flight, a limo ride, a jetboat ride, etc. A side effect of this was that they became adventurist spirits and love the outdoors. They travel a lot, drive and race cars and motorbikes, scuba dive and do a few other adventurous things. I so love the beautiful young people they have all become. I believe there is beauty in everyone!

Self-Worth

Yes, I did contemplate suicide, but as odd as it sounds that was for my children. If I'm gone then it's over, no more worries, just memories of me!

But I couldn't bear the thought of their sorrow and grief—and maybe it was the coward's way out, considering what my wife went through.

I have compensated for that by promising them their inheritance now, if they need it.

I wanted to see it benefit their lives if they needed it now, instead of waiting for me to die in who knows how many months or years, but mostly it was for me to see it work for them—selfish, I know! I am very glad I didn't go through with it, as my relationship with my children is very healthy and I love them all so much!

I guarantee you are loved and cherished by someone, but what is important is that you love and cherish yourself!

Go out and feel . . . you must change your physicality, your environment, be it as simple as having a hot shower with music that you love on in the background. Music is magic and can change your mood all by itself. Then put on a change of clothes.

But try and go out if you are able!

Memories

My goal in writing this book is to entertain you with true experiences and hopefully some funny anecdotes. The focus is on quality, not quantity. I am grateful for a good life with much to look back on, so here goes. I will start from now and go backwards . . . some memories are very vivid and others not so much.

I was diagnosed in 2019 with a nasopharyngeal (involving the sinuses and throat) tumour a little smaller than a golf ball under my left eye, with no symptoms except for occasional bleeding down the back of my throat. Fresh blood only in the morning, no disfigurement in the face, no pain.

My doctor referred me to an ear, nose and throat (ENT) specialist and I had scans and a biopsy to confirm what he thought it was. I went to an oncologist for chemotherapy and was then referred to a radiation oncologist. I went through comprehensive radiation therapy (34 treatments) and minimal chemotherapy, which I didn't tolerate due to a pre-existing heart condition.

Any woman worth her salt would have traded me in by now!

Looking Back

I did the eulogy for both mum and dad. We lost dad when he was 90, and mum at 87. It's at funerals that we look back on a loved one's life. They are gone and not in pain, not suffering anymore. It is we who are left that feel pain, suffering and sorrow.

Memories can be very powerful. For some of us it may be a song or piece of music, a beautiful smell or many things that were a part of that person's life and your relationship with them. Having lost them, life is like a jigsaw puzzle with a loving piece missing and you can't get it back! Make them proud of you by living a good life ... Kind and giving, totally loving with empathy and caring, but also protect yourself and walk away if you need to. "Ask questions without making statements," a wise man once said!

Cancer does the same thing as funerals; it makes you look back. It gave me a kick up the backside, to say "Get on with your life!" There is nothing to be gained by resentment, hate, or judging others. You can't change the past! Really, I hear that all the time! But I say yes, you *can* change the past, sometimes with one single word or sentence, or with a hug. Sometimes, you don't have a clear view of what happened or why that situation evolved. Ask them, why did they feel that way?

You can't control that person's feelings; if they can't forgive, that's their choice and often their loss!

The Pandemic

"The Pandemic Year" of 2020 didn't exist for me; I was either at appointments or in bed. I lost 30 kilos. Remember what I said about blessings? I had been a diabetic since 1990—no more diabetes! The primary tumour spawned three tumours in the lungs; the chemo took care of them, leaving me with a benign nodule in my left lung - a good result! I first asked if they could cut the primary tumour out, but its location involved too many important internal structures nearby.

I chose to ignore it as much as possible; as I said, a kick up the backside and "'adaptability to change'." I had already been doing volunteer work since retirement but had to stop due to treatment. I have since volunteered in a wildlife sanctuary feeding orphaned joeys—another wonderful experience with nature!

I have been a volunteer radio producer at a community radio station since retiring in 2016. It was a very satisfying departure from the norm, so I continued with that position. I love the fact that we are worldwide. I even get phone calls from Canada and India, and emails from all over the world. A big hi to Hans and Karine in Norway, who always email me on a Saturday night. Having been a medic in the army, I'm proud to be a member of the "Invictus family" and I always choose a song for all my courageous Invictus family members (serving and non-serving) all over the world.

I had been driving for People Who Care, an Australian volunteer-based organisation that offers community support, taking infirm patients to appointments, etc. Unfortunately, I couldn't continue with that; I loved that job! While driving for People Who Care I was taking a gentleman to an appointment. He was 4' 11" in height, and I found out that he had been a radio operator in a Lancaster bomber during the war. My dad had been a Royal Marine during the war, so we had a lot to talk about. I had asked about his height, because there was a minimum and maximum height for the army. He said his stature was an advantage in an aircraft, which made sense. I asked him where he'd met his wife, who was 4' 9" in height. He told me at a dance between missions. What are the chances?

After about my third trip with him, he invited me in to meet his lovely wife. With my cuppa we looked through some war memorabilia. The radio operator doubled as one of the gunners as well. We talked about "The Dam Busters" and other actions. I had read a lot of dad's war books, which he had accumulated. It was such a waste of life; no one wins in war!

I've applied to be a radio operator with Marine Rescue Whitfords. I need to do an induction course in September, first. I had done three shifts at Marine Rescue Mandurah before my cruise.

During that time, we had four scuba divers in distress after their boat drifted five kilometres. Anyone who knows anything about diving knows there is supposed to be a dive master on deck at all times in case anything goes wrong. All four of these divers went down! The boat drifted and luckily one of the divers had his mobile phone in a sealed bag; after swimming ashore he phoned his wife, who phoned the police, who phoned sea rescue.

Our two boats and the police launch were deployed. It's no joke . . . these idiots should have been fined big time! Anyone who puts others' lives at risk by breaking the rules should be penalised. There were three boat crews out looking for them that day in rough weather! They had made it ashore, but didn't know where they were . . .

Volunteer work allows you to control how much time, how many days and hours you can do, depending on your personal situation! You must move forward or at least regain some of your old life, or part of it!

CRUISING

I love going on cruises! In 2017, with support from my wife Sue, I left on a 35-day cruise using some of my inheritance money. I promised to take my wife to Hawai'i but she refused, saying that she could not get insurance as she had breast and metastatic liver cancer. She had already been to Maui, Hawai'i several years before I'd met her, and loved it. She died the night before I left. Feeling very lost and upset, the ocean was the best place for me to be.

Sue asked me to leave six months before, so we weren't together when I left. We hadn't had a fight and no bad feelings towards each other. I like to think it was because she knew the end was near. She wanted her ashes to be scattered in the waters of Maui.

I chose this 35-day cruise firstly because it went to Hawai'i, Tahiti, New Zealand and Western Samoa, but also because a cruise that long wouldn't have many children on board, if any. I have been on shorter cruises billed as family cruises on bigger ships—my mistake. These ships are set up like an amusement park for kids. I go on the ocean to experience peace and tranquillity! There was a curfew for the children; guess what time? Midnight! They would run up and down the corridors, push all the buttons on the lifts. It's like going outside and never looking up at the stars; my fault entirely for expecting something different.

My cruise on the 2000-passenger *Sea Princess* was brilliant. It started really well; on the first night I won the blackjack tournament and the $400 first prize! I didn't play again the whole cruise. Our first stop after our Sydney departure was Brisbane, Australia. (Some of you reading this book are not from Australia, of course, so this is for clarity.)

I didn't feel normal for about two weeks after Sue's passing and I still think of her and miss her, but her death was a "blessing" as I explained earlier. She had been in increasing pain and had to take more and more morphine elixir. She was so brave and endured over five years of chemotherapy! It worked for a while; she had eight different types. Olivia Newton John had survived for over 30 years. Don't ever give up! I'm in remission—limbo—and there will be a cure sometime. Limbo is nowhere, so don't give it any energy; ignore it!

My happy place was on deck six on the port side. At certain times of the day, it was very quiet. I would lay on a deck chair listening to my music and occasionally snoozing. The ship's movement created a gentle breeze. Sometime during the month there would be a full moon, but the ships lights were too strong and took away some of the magic of the full moon. I always arranged my mealtime to try and see the sunset. There's something magical about the sunrise and sunset at sea.

Some surprising things happened on the cruise. Almost everyone on such a long trip were retirees and pensioners, therefore over 60 and even older. One of the lovely people at my formal dining table was a woman of the world who was a cruising veteran. She was up at the crack of dawn and sat on her balcony, alert to all the goings-on around her.

At dinner that night she reported to our table that one of our passengers had died and had been taken away by ambulance that morning. Every now and then you would hear of the medical team being called to a cabin. Another seven people died on that cruise. Every cruise ship has a doctor and a morgue. Keep in mind it wasn't the ship's fault. Every cruise is a happy place with happy people.

Western Samoa

We then sailed to Western Samoa. I didn't get off the ship because all that was there for the passengers was a marketplace. I had been to Vanuatu and other Pacific islands before.

Then a 5-day cruise to our first stop in Hawai'i.

Three stops in Hawai'i and the first thing some of the women wanted to do was to go to Walmart. I couldn't believe it!

Hawai'ian Islands

Island of Hawai'i/The Big Island

I visited Kīlauea volcano on the Big Island; it always active and we could see some of the lava from the observatory. There are three craters, one inside the other. From memory, the outer crater is 3 km long by 2.5 km wide. My timing was good, because a year later it erupted, with over 450 earth tremors a day! The eruption caused fissures away from the main volcano, as a new magma chamber opened up near a housing development.

Another of my excursions took in a lava tube—fascinating stuff. I also went to a Kona coffee factory, one which supplies coffee to most of Polynesia. I couldn't believe how many blends there were; I tried some samples—absolute magic!

O'ahu

Next, onward to O'ahu and Pearl Harbour. There was a very well set up visitors' centre, but on that day it was raining and they had a lightning strike in the water between the visitors centre and the memorial of the *Arizona*. All ferries and tours were temporarily cancelled, and so therefore no trip to the *Missouri*. I had no desire to visit the gravesite of 1177 sailors; the sombre atmosphere at Pearl Harbour was enough. However, the history was very potent and real. There was a surviving sailor, a 94-year-old, with whom everyone could shake hands and say "Thank you for your service," and that made it even more real!

Maui

On to magical Maui, and another excursion. I took a bus trip to my second volcano—Haleaka. It took two hours on a not-so-straight road. The volcano crater rim stood at 10,023 feet and because of that and a long-standing heart condition I had to be sure I was not going to be compromised at altitude for a sustained length of time as it could cause a distraction for the group. So I booked a parachute jump in Australia one week before my cruise date of departure.

For that jump, I told them I wanted to jump from 10,000 feet. We got to 10,000 and I was told that no one was jumping from that height, so we went to 12,000., the pilot yelled out 2 miles! No one jumped … five jumpers in the plane, so we went to 14,000 ft. Breathing was noticeably a little harder, but the heart was fine, no palpitations, which would mean that the heart is in distress. There was no wind that day, which would make a difference to the landing. With wind, you land into the wind, and almost walk on landing.

They teach you to land with your legs straight out in front of you. I landed flat on my backside with a thump, bruising my coccyx. It took three weeks to heal, so I spent my first two weeks of the cruise sitting sideways, changing from one cheek to the other. If anything goes wrong, always listen to the expert!

Still, it was a great experience doing my first parachute jump. I investigated doing a jump in Hawai'i but it was quite expensive, so I was very happy to see the beautiful countryside from a tourist coach. Some intriguing facts about Hawai'i—the alphabet has only 16 letters, and it didn't become a part of the United States of America until 1959. It has become one of my favourite places, it is so beautiful, and the people are so friendly! I plan on going back in the future!

Kaua'i

Onto the next island of Kaua'i; this is the northernmost of the seven main Hawai'ian islands. After docking I caught a cab with a group that were heading off to Walmart! I stayed with the cab and asked the driver if there was a tourist heliport somewhere nearby. When we had left the ship, we'd turned left; he said the heliport was just near the harbour, but to the right.

There were six helicopters, all booked out, and they told me there was an hour and a half wait. I had nothing else to do, so I waited. I was on a flight within 40 minutes as someone had cancelled. The flight was an hour long, and worth every cent. It was all captured by four cameras on each 'copter, to be given to you on a USB drive as a memory of your flight! These helicopters were the ones used in the 2015 *Jurassic World* movie; they were very exotic and very safe.

The island of Kaua'i was owned by a British gentleman who on his death bequeathed the entire island to the Hawai'ian people, so that no one would ever be homeless. What a magnificent gesture!

On Kaua'i I also visited my third volcano. Yes, I'm fascinated by volcanoes, having seen three in New Zealand when I was in my mid-twenties: Ruapehu, Tongariro (both active volcanoes) and Mount Egmont, an extinct volcano. All of these were on the North Island. New Zealand should be on your bucket list, if it isn't already.

In Kaua'i, the helicopter flew into the half-million-year-old extinct volcano crater. The pilot, a Hawai'ian gent who was a great commentator, mentioned that there was normally a waterfall flowing over the crater wall, as this was the second wettest place on the planet. He did a great job throughout the flight.

We flew through a light rain shower, but that was it. Helicopters aren't as affected by the weather as fixed-wing planes.

We flew over the surfing spot where a courageous young surfer lost her arm to a tiger shark. We flew near Julia Robert's $17 million house, that she had just sold, and Pierce Brosnan's house, both of which had restricted air space—they deserve their privacy!

I highly recommend a helicopter flight as a way to see and experience the beauty of this magnificent island! I missed Sue not being there to share all this with me. She loved Hawai'i! She did her first and only helicopter flight with me in Esperance, West Australia. She sat with the pilot—always a great way to see everything, especially over islands and beaches.

Tahiti

We had three stops in Tahiti: Bora Bora, the city of Papeete on the Island of Tahiti, and Moorea.

Bora Bora

At Bora Bora we were docked next to Rupert Murdoch's three-masted yacht. I went to our top deck (thirteenth, from memory) and looked up—his centre mast was taller than our ship! Wow! I was told it had 11 permanent crew on board. On the far side was James Packer's super yacht, very modern—quite a contrast!

It was a very pleasant place with $400-a-night chalets over the water, which is what everyone comes here for, along with the lovely turquoise waters and pristine beaches.

A beautiful place, very romantic; I noticed lots of Americans here.

Moorea

At Moorea I had booked to go "swimming with sharks." It's not as dangerous as it sounds. Our ship was anchored in a deep-water channel. In the distance was the mountain peak that was used in the movie *South Pacific*, and also in the Marlon Brando version of *Mutiny on the Bounty*.

We were informed that Brando's Island, which he bought way back when he married a native Tahitian lady, was now a totally private sanctuary that is rented out at $7,000 per night with a minimum of three nights required. Apparently, it is "used by a lot of celebrities" as it is very private and secure!

We were picked up by a Tahitian charter boat with a crew of four. They took us to a lagoon on the other side of the island, which was a very pleasant trip. We anchored in about one metre of water and were invited to jump in. There were white tip reef sharks ranging to about 4' in length and sting rays about 3' to 4' across.

They were all very tame and very comfortable with humans as they knew they were about to be hand fed. It was very amusing watching the rays, they would actually hug the crew member feeding them. The sharks were fed about 50' away to ensure there was no competition. They appear to live in perfect harmony in their little part of the world.

Keeping in mind that we were snorkelling, it was still unnerving when one of the sharks passed under one of us, and there was an occasional scream from one of the children when one of the sharks ventured too close out of curiosity. Everyone was briefed before entering the water—don't put your hand near the shark's mouths, but of course there is always one! He wasn't on my boat but only received a minor wound. I imagine they could do some damage if provoked. It was certainly "a great and wonderful close encounter with nature."

I had also booked a shark cage experience hoping to meet a "great white" up close. They are a warm-blooded shark and are found in every ocean in the world. Only two of two thousand passengers booked that; I understand the fear, but the staff would not let anything happen to you. It didn't happen as it wasn't worth their while to only take one person out and the other client cancelled. I should have paid for both of us, whether they came or not. It would have been cheaper, as we don't do it out of Perth. It's on my bucket list—a once in a lifetime venture. You don't travel to *not* do things.

All tropical islands are magical, the ultimate in nature—warm with soft summer breezes! In 35 days, we never hit any bad weather; the navigator whose job it is to find the best way around lows and bad weather did a brilliant job. My cabin was at the front of the ship, and you could hear the waves gently hit the hull during the night. It was almost always windy but mostly pleasant in the tropical air.

When we were anchored in Papeete, on returning by tender boat to the ship the wind had picked up and therefore the swell had increased in size. When trying to get 40 people off the boat with us bobbing up and down, we struck the side of the *Sea Princess* and cracked the side of the tender boat's hull. Everyone was frantic to get a couple who were just married that day in Papeete off the boat first.

We all survived, but it's incredible what a small swell is capable of.

New Zealand

What an incredibly beautiful place! I had lived in Napier, on the east coast of the North Island, for eight months on the way to the Montreal Olympics back in 1976.

Two stops here, the city of Auckland and the Bay of Islands region. I don't have a lot to say here; Auckland is another beautiful city to visit. We left that night and were told that we wouldn't be going to Bay of Islands due to a 7-metre swell, not allowing the tender boats to be lowered. I'm glad not to have gone through that. Although as you've probably noticed, it is the extremes in life that you remember the most!

This was in 2017, long before the eruption that killed 22 people on White Island in December 2019.

I know a lot of Kiwis (a well-known nickname for New Zealanders), and say to them how beautiful their country is, and ask "So why are you all over here in Perth, the farthest point away from Kiwi land?" —with a smile on my face, of course; I know why they're here! They are such easy-going people! I love my Kiwi friends.

HOME

Onward to Sydney, Australia. Most cruises time their arrival to go through the heads in daylight; it's something very special to see! We unfortunately had a medical emergency en route; we were told we were supposed to be met by a helicopter to airlift the patient, but that the distance was too far. So we increased speed, and arrived at 2 a.m. It doesn't make sense to me, but that's what we were told.

I would do that cruise again, but the *Sea Princess* has been sold. It was the perfect size with the perfect number of passengers. Thanks, mum and dad, for the gift of a magical cruise; love you! They say that whenever you think of a deceased loved one, their spirit is drawn to you, and they are standing right beside you. True or not it is very comforting; I choose to believe it!

There is much more to tell but I will leave you with only one more story from the cruise. Each evening meal you had the choice to sit at the allocated dining table, usually an enjoyable experience. Almost all the staff were from the Philippines and were very polite and efficient at their jobs. Many were away from their families for seven months or more at a time.

One gentleman at our table who thought he was better than everyone else would say something derogatory to the waiter, and then say, "You don't know what that means, do you?" I replied on the waiter's behalf by saying "Wow. I'll bet he knows more English than you know Filipino!" He shut up from that point on, receiving a glare from his wife!

There's always one!

Everyone should read a book on genetics. There are reasons why we look and speak differently. It always makes me laugh when a person persecutes a dark-skinned person. So, you go and lie on the beach why? Oh . . . to get a tan . . .

Humans are organisms that adapt to their environment. Australian Aboriginals don't lose salt in their sweat; the Kalahari Bushmen of Africa can go without water for up to three days. They also have two eye lids to protect their eyes. People with big lips are usually from a hot climate and conversely people with thin lips are usually from a cold climate—or their ancestors were. Of course, genetics from past generations plays a large part in your physical characteristics and appearance—your strongest protective genes will be passed on to your children!

ATTITUDE

There are a lot of things in life that change your thinking and attitudes.

Sometimes it's certain people—what they say and do! The actors Keanu Reeves and Sandra Bullock fall into this category, as well as Tom Hardy and many others. They are very grateful for the luck they have had, the talent they have; they are very giving and humble, treating others with love and respect and not expecting anything in return.

Thank you for being such shining examples of the human spirit! Every form of caring is a form of love!

Nature can do that for us too. Someone once asked me what my favourite animal was. My reply was a condor. Not because it is majestic but because it is free and values life. Look at where it lives—the view, the majesty of its surroundings. It experiences the "circle of life." So beautiful!

It only takes what it needs, as does most of nature. It, like most animals, will defend to the death its young.

Travel

We have four weeks annual leave in Australia. I booked a trip to Europe during my years at the hospital, when I was single.

I flew to Athens, Greece, and stayed overnight at a beautiful place with a roof garden. At three o'clock in the morning I went up there and was met with the wonderful sight of Athens in the glow of city lights. The next day I went on a tour of this majestic historic city—Australia has 200 years of colonial history; Europe has 2,000 years. Back then you were able to walk among the ruins of the Acropolis. From memory, the Acropolis is on one of five hills on which Athens was built.

I then caught a coach to Zeebrugge, Belgium, a four-day trip. On leaving Athens, the road was marked with crosses where people had lost their lives in car accidents—not a bad idea to remind everyone of the dangers of the roads! We went through the old Yugoslavia. Some buildings still had bullet holes in the walls—all of this region had been through the Second World War. Only two domestic animals (two cats) were seen in all the time driving through that part of Europe. On through Germany and France, the food was wonderful. The Autobahn was an experience.

I caught the hovercraft from Zeebrugge, Belgium to Dover; what a sight it was seeing the White Cliffs of Dover, iconic with such history. Imagine what it was like for the pilots returning from missions during the war. It must have been a welcoming sight of home. Mum and dad gave me a list of relatives to see and if

I had done that I wouldn't have had time to do anything else. I didn't go to Stonehenge—my one regret!

After that, I left the UK and returned to see the rest of Europe. Switzerland was awesome! I left Zurich in the rain and took a coach up through the clouds to a restaurant at 8,000 ft opposite The Eiger, a famous mountain. I sat there with my coffee under the clear blue sky reading *The Eiger Sanction*, having seen the Clint Eastwood film of the same name. You could see the mountain chain that is the Alps—magnificent! I'm so grateful to have had the opportunity do all those things.

Work

My army days were certainly character building! You learned to be self-sufficient and adapt to any situation. But don't be too cocky, as I learned when I went to rescue a twelve-year-old girl who was drowning.

I was with my girlfriend and a group of friends at this swimming hole, when this girl got into trouble. I am not a strong swimmer and didn't know of any rescue techniques, but I went in to try to save her. In a panic she wrapped me up as soon as I was within reach, and we went under. We were in about eight feet of water. They say you see your life flash before your eyes, but that didn't happen to me.

I felt the soft sand between my toes, I saw the sunlight filtering through the surface of the water and after the initial panic there was an incredible peace. I went unconscious, and the next thing I awoke on the shore, having been rescued by an off-duty lifeguard. He rescued her first, and then me—luckily, I suffered no brain damage! They say if you have a near death experience, you are closer to the spirit world. I don't care if you believe me, but there have been things that have happened to protect me!

As I may have mentioned, I've had a somewhat fractured work life. Being a medic in the army led me to almost everything in my work life being involved in the medical field. My mother, having been a nurse during the war, worked in a hospital and so I fell into a position at her hospital as a theatre orderly. Possibly because they knew I had just come out of the army as a medic, I was permitted to watch some of the operations after the patient had been draped. I worked in the theatre for five years and then in the ward for four years.

We had a maternity ward and would do on average two caesareans a week. Over five years that's about 500 cases, and definitely more as most babies won't wait for the 7 to 3.30 shift. My role was to drag the bodies of the fainted husbands and partners out of the theatre. They were told not to look at the reflection in the glass of the light source. There are many things I could tell you about, some very sad, some quite unique. But the joy of the new parents overtook everything!

When I went to the ward, I met a gentleman who was at Gallipoli (mainly significant to Australians and New Zealanders). He told me how close he came to death when a shell had landed and exploded in front of him, showering and burying him with dirt. Only his hand showed through, and his mates dug him out. He also said that the enemy forces had placed barbed wire just under the surface of the water at the landing beach, impeding the advance of the Australian and New Zealand troops. He said the sea was red for a mile out from the blood of the dead, wounded and dying. We had some great conversations, having both been in the military, as I would sit with him every chance I had. He left not long after in reasonable health. What a lovely man.

Before working at the hospital, I planned a trip to the Montreal Olympics in 1976. My girlfriend and I left in December of 1975 to go to New Zealand. We lived in Napier on the east coast of the North Island. I got a job at a bakery and my girlfriend worked in an accountant's office. We were there for almost eight months. Dad shipped my car over and we drove around the island every chance we had. There were lots of special things to see and experience on the North Island—the beautiful Lake Taupō;

Rotorua, with its geysers and hot mud pools; Mount Tongariro and Mount Ruapehu, both active volcanoes; Mount Egmont, an extinct volcano; and the lush plains and grasslands. We didn't make it to Montreal, Canada as we'd spent all our savings in New Zealand.

I loved New Zealand! Apart from the weather it was very much like Hawai'i. I went back two years later to the South Island by myself and did everything by coach, one of the best ways to see the countryside unless you have a car and you can go off the beaten track.

New Zealand was so lush and green. If you love nature, New Zealand is the place for your adventure. There were snow-capped mountains, volcanic mud pools, volcanoes, glaciers—I flew onto the Fox Glacier and did the Shotover River jet boat experience, what a ride! —and no snakes. Australia has almost 200 species of snakes, and over 30 of the world's most poisonous snakes.

After working at the hospital came the opportunity to work as a first aid instructor for the Australian Red Cross. It's amazing how superstitious some people are. They believed they would attract negative first-aid situations into their lives; true or not, wouldn't you rather be prepared. They were usually thinking of some random event on the street, not about someone close to them. We did a summertime course called "dial a young life," which was three hours after work, specifically for people with swimming pools. I had some residents who would not participate but would sit and watch. I can only think that it would be fear that would be the cause of this, because they all had children. Sadly, we had a lot of pool drownings that year.

Training helps and kicks in on its own. "ABC"—that's how simple it is: Airway, Breathing, Circulation. But you need to know what to do if the "ABC" is compromised. Please go and do a first aid course! I have been involved in four resuscitations in my entire life; three of the people survived. The oldest was 74, the youngest was 31. Guess which one didn't survive? You don't have to be the only factor, and symptoms are varied! Unless you've had an echocardiogram you have no idea what state your heart is in.

I had a heart attack last year with no symptoms before going unconscious. Luckily, I was at a dance class with two lovely nurses in the group who looked after me until the ambulance arrived. My cardiologist said if I had been alone at home I might not be here now. Very lucky! I had atrial fibrillation, apparently quite common. But I already had cardiomyopathy; my left ventricle didn't work properly; therefore three chambers weren't working properly. My pulse was 160 beats per minute while I was unconscious.

The specialist said, "The heart is a muscle; it will eventually get tired and stop." The ambulance got there within ten minutes and stabilised me before taking me for a three-day stay at the hospital, after two attempts at cardioversion that didn't work. Afterwards I was asked to attend a lecture on medication and other things relevant. There were 15 participants and not one of us had the same symptoms before our heart attack. It is quite often referred pain; down the arm, in the jaw, in the back etc., and breathing difficulties. Don't mess around, call an ambulance if needed!

Papua New Guinea

The Red Cross sent me to Papua New Guinea to do a first aid course in Goroka, in the Eastern Highlands Province of Papua New Guinea.

They flew me to Melbourne, Australia—I live in Perth—for a briefing of the culture and the do's and don'ts as a representative of the Red Cross. I have always been very proud to wear the uniform of the Red Cross! I was flown to Port Moresby and was met by Cosmos, the right-hand man of the CEO. I met and stayed at the CEO's house that night and flew to Goroka the next day. Almost all the ex-pats have dogs and a barbed wire fence around their house. This was in the 1980s and there had been many muggings and robberies.

On arrival in Goroka I had afternoon tea with a doctor who ran a six-bed hospital there and was the head of the research facility. They were the best in the world at that time for malaria research. As you can imagine, anywhere in the tropics is prone to that disease. I was told to wear long pants and long-sleeved shirts. One night I watched a very persistent mosquito trying to bite through my jeans. He was trying to get his proboscis between the threads of the denim. I swatted him before he had time to do any damage. Tenacious little bugger!

Before I left Australia, I had started taking anti-malarial drugs. On the tour of the hospital in Goroka I told the doc what I was taking. He said, "That takes care of four strains." I asked how many there are. Twenty-two! Perhaps this is why over three million people worldwide still die from malaria.

The Australian Air Force had a training base there in Goroka, and like Singapore, the weather closed in at 2 p.m. every day. Every mountain in Papua New Guinea, I am told, is named after the first pilot that crashed into it—no joke!

My students and I were put up in a Lutheran boarding house for the two-week course. The house was run by two lovely ladies who looked after us diligently. Some of the villagers would go into the jungle early in the morning to collect fresh fruit for breakfast. How different the bananas and other fruit tasted, compared to our commercially grown fruit here in Australia.

I had two local police officers from the Asawa tribe (sometimes known as "The Mud People") on my first aid course. Both were well-educated, well-spoken, intelligent and very knowledgeable about the ways of the jungle. They jokingly told me about a tree whose "sap" when rubbed on my dry shirt would kill me when it was absorbed by my sweaty skin! They both passed the course with flying colours. I also had a scuba instructor named Diane. She and her husband ran a diving business in Port Moresby, taking ex-pats on diving excursions. The weekend before I returned to Australia, I spent the night with them. Diane took me to the local swimming pool to familiarise me with the scuba equipment and to provide a short briefing on the dangers of the depths.

We had dived on a small circular reef; what I remember of that was that the water was very warm and we went to one atmosphere (approximately 33 ft). I was dressed in my jeans and a flannel shirt because I was told it could get cold at depth. There were three of us "first timers" swimming behind her. We swam in single file, but none of us wanted to be at the end of line.

When I was in the army, I'd met some soldiers from a "stevedore unit," the water division of the army. They had worked in Papua New Guinea and had set a baited hook off a drum line. They caught a 19-foot-long tiger shark, but before they had a chance to get to it, a bite had been taken out of it with a bite radius greater than that of the hooked tiger shark—scary! One reef shark was spotted that day. Diane led us and looked after us while we spent half an hour swimming around the reef. We did two dives that day—another great experience with nature. I was always fascinated by scuba diving, as they say it's the closest you can get to weightlessness, and I love anything to do with space!

All the wildlife in the tropics is usually big and wants to eat you! You have to be a little careful. I was very intrigued by the spiders in Goroka. They would actually work together to catch prey. For example, the distance between lampposts is 22 yards (one chain). The spiders (maybe 20 of them) would interconnect their webs between two lampposts. You didn't see them during the day, but at dusk they all came out. I was told that they sometimes caught small birds, their webs were so strong. I had heard some time ago of spider's webs in the Amazon that would cut your skin if you walked into them.

On my final day I stayed at Diane and hubby's place. I was up early and got myself a coffee and sat, just me and the dog, on their veranda in the brightening dawn. Their place was built into the side of a hill with the veranda hanging over the river water. In the still morning with fish jumping out of the water, it was pure heaven! Those are Memories I'll treasure forever - I felt at peace!

Flying

I'll go back for a bit, it's sort of related to space . . . I started getting my pilot's licence shortly after getting out of the Army, in the mid-1970s. There was only me at the time, so no responsibilities.

I went solo in a Cessna 150 at 11 hours or training average, I'm told. We'd finished a training session and I landed. My instructor asked me to turn off the taxiway and he got out. I was going solo! Daunting, but exciting. The progression of flying exercises was fun except for the "wing-dip stall" that scared the hell out of me! Normal flying is straight and level. A stall is controllable, but when your wing dips you are not level and therefore can overturn and go out of control. It sure changes your point of reference, which is the ground.

I also had one landing incident with the incoming sea breeze that we here in Perth call the "Fremantle Doctor." The circuit is always anti-clockwise and I was turning onto final approach. Just as I turned with the wings tilted down the wind hit and blew me sideways. Scared the willies out of me, and I had to do a go-round; I landed safely with my knees shaking uncontrollably. I loved flying (like a condor) but it was too expensive after they doubled the price of aviation fuel—AVGAS as it's known. I hope to fly again, it is total freedom!

One thing they teach you is that if an object is coming at you from the side and the angle stays the same you are going to collide. I saw a black dot out of the corner of my eye. It was an eagle! I was flying at 3,000 ft on the way to the training area.

We got close enough that I could see his eyes before he dived away. I know of a crash over the Serengeti in Africa after hitting a vulture that buckled the wing of a Cessna. The pilot survived.

My flying training gave me a real appreciation for pilots who fly in the outback. I was flown to a work site by one. BHP Mining got wind of my presence doing a first aid course, and I was requested to add on a one-week course at the Ok Tedi copper mine site. They flew me in and we landed in a twin engine plane on a grass strip—a little bit hairy and bumpy, but our Australian pilot did a fabulous job. Apparently, a lot of Australian pilots get jobs there to get training in some very trying conditions and having to adapt to outback conditions with limited radio reception and all types of landing and take-off dynamics, including changing weather.

No roads existed at that time of the mine opening, and all of its equipment was dismantled at sea level and flown up there by helicopter. Roads and buildings were built, and the Fly River was the closest avenue for shipping their supplies from some 70 km away. They had a drought just before I arrived, and supplies were affected; the main concern was a shortage of beer! It was the general belief that keeping alcohol in the blood protected them against malaria (that may or may not be true). The big concern from management was that the workforce turned to hard liquor, and for good reason, as they had just had their first murder! There were no rules back then about blood-alcohol levels on site.

Most of the workforce were very hard-working Koreans. The entire class had 100% pass. Considering English was their second language, that was really good! I've also worked for Rio Tinto, and people whine about the safety regulations. The regulations are annoying but necessary—almost all accidents on site are fatal, and often caused by not following the rules.

Healing Work

As I mentioned earlier, I had felt like a lost soul for many years, and I didn't know why. The brain shuts painful memories out. The reason was that I had been molested at nine years of age by a drunk in a phone booth, back in the days when kids played outside until the sun went down. I only found out after regressive therapy hypnosis, at age 33. It had affected me all my life, but knowing why has helped from that point on. I then became a phlebotomist ("bloodsucker" as we say jokingly) taking blood samples in the field—a mobile phlebotomist, specialising in warfarin patients and meeting some sick but wonderful people.

I sometimes had time to talk and hear about their lives and what they had been through with their illness and treatment. The majority were heart and cancer patients. I refuse to use the words "sufferer" or "victim" Most were very upbeat and coped really well; their attitude was "it is what it is!" The medical profession does its best to deal with people's symptoms but there are so many types of cancer so finding a cure is quite hard. But we're getting there, hopefully! What I learned from these lovely people was to listen. One patient thanked me for doing her bleed from where she asked of me, she said some people won't listen and think they know better. Taking blood from warfarin patients is very painful, and I always tried to get it in the first try.

I recall one incident taking blood from a bikie at one of our centres. Isn't it funny how some people can't handle the site of blood, especially their own blood? This gentleman fainted and the concern was that he might have a gun in his boot. He came to, and we looked after him for as long as necessary and then he left, very appreciative.

Onward to being a bus driver for Transperth; no two days were ever the same. I had one accident in three years. I partly caused a six-kilometre traffic jam during the morning peak hour. I was heading to my first terminus for the start of the day, and therefore had no passengers. As I was going through a set of traffic lights with a car waiting to turn across me, the lights turned amber just at that spot where you are in no-man's land. I actually put my hand up to tell him to stay put. I had the "banana bus," all 18 tons of it, and it's not easy to stop. We are trained to not brake hard so we don't have passengers flying all over the place. As I'm going through the intersection, he comes across me. You know that concept where they say that things go in slow motion? Well, bits of the car flew up in the air in front of me. He luckily was ok, his car wasn't! The front of his car was under the bus. We both were taken to hospital to be checked out.

I had one incident that I had to laugh at; in training, they teach you that if you feel lost, ask your passengers to help out. This is when you are just going solo. They like to start you in the afternoon shift going through to midnight or later. Early evening on a Friday night, I had only two teenagers on board. At a T-junction I was supposed to go left, but the boys said no, to the right is the way. Well, guess what next stop was? Right outside of McDonalds, didn't I feel the fool!

I left that job to go to the mining industry driving dump trucks (known as haulpaks). Up at 4.30 in the morning, and a half-hour drive to the site for a twelve-hour shift. It's an alien environment to city folk. A driller in the pit had been struck on his safety boot by a death adder snake, very hard to see in the rocks.

My first mine site job was Lanfranchi, a "decline" mine where you drive underground on a circular road. I was a first aid/safety officer and had my one and only casualty from an unfortunate incident. He was scaling the walls downchiselling the odd rocks poking out of the walls. A section of the wall came away with him and going down the mill hole, where they tip the ore to a central point for collection. He tumbled about 100 ft. I went down with the mine boss in his mine vehicle. We almost had a head-on crash with a vehicle bringing him to the surface. I had already instructed them not to move him due to the possibility of spinal injuries. When I assessed him in the first aid room, I carefully ran my fingers down his spine. He said, "oh my god, I didn't think of that!" I said, "That's why I'm the first aid officer." We were being watched by three union reps. They came in the next day asking why didn't I transport him straight away. He had been in shock and apart from a few scrapes and a possible broken wrist, he needed to be stabilised. I met another ambulance halfway a few hours later and transferred him, wanting to be away from my site for the absolute minimum amount of time.

Years later in a different role, I was driving a 270-ton haulpak with a maximum load of 260 tons. You could drive it with your little finger. It was left-hand drive, worth four million dollars. The front tyres were one hundred thousand each, rears sixty thousand each. Sue was diagnosed while I was doing my training. I couldn't sleep and therefore couldn't concentrate, making many mistakes and eventually getting the sack as I was a danger to others. They did the right thing!

I did odd driving jobs until mum died in 2016 and I received my inheritance. I was glad to be volunteering at Curtin Radio as a producer and driving for People Who Care, a very worthwhile detour from my feeling of loss of my parents and my wife. Being a producer for a community radio is a real privilege.

I also volunteer with a wildlife sanctuary looking after orphaned joeys, which is a very special experience. They all have names; I will tell you about one in particular. His name is Rambo, so named because of his courage. He was found after two days in the sun on a 40-degree day, on a fire break in the sand. He was estimated to be six weeks old. He was later found to be blind due to the sunlight exposure. He also had burns and a sunburn as he didn't have any fur yet. They are all so cute and generally do what they are told, but not always. We look after 26 joeys at the moment. Almost all of their mothers were roadkill.

I have applied to volunteer at Marine Rescue Whitfords as a radio operator. I have used radios in the air training corps, the army as a medic, as a trainee pilot, and finally in the mining industry driving haulpaks. I would highly recommend the Air Training Corp cubs, scouts, even the military for personal and character development. But follow your heart and intuition! Don't do anything if it feels wrong!

Bee Sting

Let's start at the beginning.

I remember being in mum's garden in England as a five-year-old and seeing a pretty colourful little thing on a flower, not knowing what it was, or how it could hurt me. It was only doing what it was put on this earth to do and go home after a day's work collecting nectar from mum's garden. In England they have a very sturdy animal called a "bumblebee." It was doing what bees do, but I picked it up and of course it stung me! It was my first memory of pain.

I remember walking to school in the cold; all the puddles had frozen over, and I took great pleasure in the cracking noise it made when I trod on it. I remember joy in my first experience of weather, but I didn't like the thunderstorms. Most homes in England have a chimney and experience many severe storms. We had survived on many occasions, but not this time. With an almighty crash our chimney ended up on our driveway, leaving a big mess to clean up. Dad being an ex-royal marine and very resourceful, managed to deal with the situation before work the next day.

My next memory was of Butlin's Holiday Camp, an absolute paradise for children. I remember being laid up for several days. Apparently, I'd come very close to drowning and after swallowing a significant amount of water, mum had pulled me out of the deep end of the pool by my hair. I later experienced drowning for real at the age of 18 while trying to save a twelve-year-old in difficulty in a lagoon in Queensland, as mentioned earlier.

Australia

My next memory was of coming to Australia.

We were "Ten Pound Poms" and had to catch a train to the port of Southampton, to get to the cruise ship *Orcades* for a three-week journey to Fremantle, Western Australia. As a six-year-old and full of adventurous spirit, I wandered down the platform at the train station and fell between the train and the platform. It wasn't a big deal for me as the train wasn't moving and I was tiny compared to the train's wheels, but mum and dad saw it differently and I incurred their wrath.

By the way, did I mention that I am a twin? I don't have any memories of my brother being in trouble . . . ever! He was firstborn; I say, "I let him out first." He was 7lb 10z and I was 5 lb 2 oz. I was told he stole my nutrients. We are not identical, which we are both thankful for.

I loved being on the ocean, even when we went through storms. I remember the waves washing over the decks. I became the quoits champion of the ship at age seven having had my birthday on board the ship. We stopped at Naples, with the glow of Mount Vesuvius (one of the most active volcanoes in the world) in the night sky. All the night shops were full of wonderful toys—absolute paradise for us kids. We went through the Suez Canal, which was quite an experience. We were able to see the Sahara Desert from the deck, and of course it was very hot and windy.

We arrived three weeks later in Fremantle, Western Australia. It was 108 degrees Fahrenheit; it was not very pleasant for us poms, never having experienced such scorching temperatures before. My dad's first words standing on the deck were "My god, what have I done!?" At that time Fremantle was mostly a railway freight yard.

We were processed as migrants and taken to Graylands hostel, a migrant transition centre, where we remained for approximately six months. Memories of that place were of the iron bed posts being too hot to touch and the hot nights during Perth's hot summertime. And a wasp's nest in the open dirt where my brother and I played! Mum and dad were building a house in an outer suburb of Perth, only called "outer" because we had market gardens behind us. We were only one of two houses built on our dirt street when we moved in.

Nature's Plan

Nature has a plan; it knows what to do. There's a concept called entrainment.

A flock of 1,000 starlings never bump into each other in flight.

A school of hundreds of fish turn at the same time without being able to see past the fish in front of them.

The consciousness that exists within the animal world is amazing.

I once heard of troops of monkeys on different islands in Japan, a story related by Tony Robbins at one of his seminars maybe 20 years ago. They had no knowledge of the other groups, but group by group they learned how to wash sweet potatoes before eating them, without seeing it done by the other groups on the other islands.

My work life was very fractured with lots of different jobs after three deaths in my family: Dad in 2015, mum in 2016 and my wife in 2017.

Which leads me to now, writing this book. I guess it's a form of closure—but I'm not ready to die just yet. I do feel melancholy sometimes . . . a lot of wasted years . . . "Honour Your Gifts." I never had the guts to follow through.

At this moment I am feeling very sad. I've just learned that a dear friend has terminal mesothelioma. She's taking it like the brave trooper that she is and living her life as normal as she can.

I love my friends! It's very important to stay in touch, it doesn't matter the time interval. Some I may not have seen or talked to for months, but it seems like I saw them yesterday. Almost everyone who is a lasting friend I have met through either tennis or dancing.

I can't do either of those things anymore. I now play chess at my library and go to a quiz night every Tuesday. I work at the radio every second Saturday and every second Wednesday. That keeps me out of mischief.

You will never meet anyone sitting in front of the TV.

It is very important to find your "happy place!"

I don't dance anymore but I still go to the dance group. The music, the people, the atmosphere, and my wonderful friends that I have got to know—that is "my happy place!" I'm sure it freaks some of the women out, this guy sitting and watching the dance class.

There are only happy people at dancing, such good vibes!

FULL CIRCLE - LIFE LESSONS

You must find your "happy place!" You must think happy thoughts. Find something that you love or an experience that you treasure and use that! Happiness changes your physicality. Just using words can do it; someone once taught me many years ago that just changing "I hate that" to "I love that" will change your thinking and possibly the outcome. Very important!

I've met a few people with cancer, some very religious—one in particular. I know I said I wouldn't talk about religion, but this is important, I think. She has been given four months to live. Dr. Bernie Seagal, author of *Love, Medicine and Miracles* said don't ever let a doctor tell you when you are going to die! She is riddled with cancer; she had no symptoms until a month ago, had scans and was diagnosed. She is at peace because of her faith; it doesn't matter what happens next!

Did you know there are over four hundred religions in the world? Which one is the right one for you? Whatever you believe is right for you!

You can't force anyone to love you, and you can't force anyone to believe in something!

May you look back with love on all the wonderful people, places and fond memories you have experienced in your life.

I like to go to a Buddhist temple for meditation now and then. The abbot has a question-and-answer session at the end of the meditation. Their philosophy is not to judge anyone, which is not easy to do. But try it! It is you who are burdened if you judge and can't forgive. The abbot—his name is Arjunbrahm (forgive me if I've misspelled your name)—is English, with a degree in theoretical physics. He's been a monk for over 30 years. He tells fabulous stories about his life as a monk. As a Buddhist you must preserve all life. In his learning years as a junior monk, he was in Thailand. He said the mosquitoes knew about those rules and took full advantage of them.

Every living thing has the right to life!

He also teaches meditation at a local prison. It's all about your mental perceptions as to how you will cope in jail. He told the congregation about a retreat where he had had no human contact for six weeks. He said it was absolute bliss! He just ate, slept and meditated, not a worry in the world!

Try and do everything you do with confidence. Just doing it that way will change your total outlook and you won't worry about what others think or do!

I only allow good people into my life, and I urge you to do the same. I also look after the people I care about. It's not that had hard to do, just be there for them!

As I said, Sue died the day before I left on the cruise; that's when you learn who are the caring people in your life. Sue had "friends" who never made contact with her again, and so did I. I can only think that it is fear . . . of morbidity, of having to look after that person while they are sick from chemo or radiation!

When I went on my 35-day cruise my DJ and friend Gordon jokingly played the song "" Six Months in a Leaky Boat" before I left. Gordon always looks after me with cakes and biscuits when I do my shifts with him. We connected almost immediately when we met, as I was a tennis umpire in my final year, doing 24 Hopman Cups and 17 Australian Opens before I got sick. It was something special to be on court with the "royalty" of the tennis world. Pat Rafter and Andre Agassi were my favourites, as well as Federer of course!

One year at the Australian Open Agassi came dressed like a pirate with a goatee and balaclava. He was followed around the whole tournament by a group of about 15 duplicates of him. So funny! He lost that year to Pete Sampras in the semi-finals but won the next year against Sampras in two brilliant five-set semi-finals. Each one went on to win the tournament. Gordon had played in junior Wimbledon as a 16-year-old. He's a lovely guy who has done a lot in his life, always with a giving heart.

So, I guess that's it . . . of course that's not everything, and I'm sorry if this book turned out to be "my memoirs." But I hope you've enjoyed my story. Everything I do from now on is for my children and grandchildren.

I wish you all the very best of love—sending hugs!

Before I go:

You will learn things about yourself—how strong and resilient you are!

You may learn your limitations.

Don't be too proud to accept help from friends and loved ones.

There are always support groups.

Stay well in spirit; your body doesn't always do what you tell it.

Stay positive as much as you can!

Stay active, be in your "happy place" as much as possible.

There is a positive concept called "planting the seed." Plant the seed of wellness in your thinking and don't worry about the outcome. What will happen will happen, but you can influence the outcome by enjoying life as much as possible. You actually feel more alive when you are sick. The Paralympics taught me that. Humans can do some amazing things when they are tested and put their minds to it.

Cry because you're happy, cry because you're sad, but feel . . .

I'm not leaving this world with any enemies, a choice I've made. I try not to judge people. And I hope to be endowed with "wisdom" as an old man when I go.

I think of myself as being young at heart. My body doesn't always listen.

I don't allow anyone to call me "sir." That puts me above them . . . we are all equal . . . and I haven't been knighted yet!

Finally: learn to be still and breathe!

Honour Your Gifts!
Be Proud of Yourself!
I'm sorry for what you are going through—Sending Love!

Acknowledgements

To all the researchers, doctors and specialists and others involved in the treatment and investigation of cancer. Thank you for all your hard work!

To all my friends who are fighting "the beast," sending much love to you!

To my good friends L and Gary who have always been there for me, especially through my illness and recovery.

To my lovely friend Dawn, who taught me how to umpire tennis—one of the great joys of my life. I loved the international flavour of the people, the world's languages . . . the Swedes would chant "we are yellow, we are blue, we are Swedish, who are you?"

To all my beautiful children, especially Kat, who challenges my thinking. She is very intuitive and we always have wonderful conversations. She is a bit of a tomboy, very positive and always moving forward in her life.

Also, David and Hayden, my two youngest boys—grown men now. Both have a beautiful spirit, although they may not see it in themselves. They are always in contact and look after me in their own way.

To my brothers and sisters, especially Tricia who is always a good listener and lovely to talk to.

Vicki, who is a long way away, but is a sincere and caring person in her own right.

My youngest brother Brian who is legally blind but has coped very well in his life with the help of a loving wife. He has always worked and provided for his family.

Finally, to those who have inspired and changed me . . .

Robin Lee Graham—when I was 21 years old, his story inspired me to travel and to buy a Surf-Cat Catamaran.

Sandra Bullock—watching you on a talk show with a picture of your adopted children. Forget about your celebrity status, what a beautiful soul you are!

Keanu Reeves—you, like Sandra, show the world how to be unselfish, empathetic, loving and without wanting anything in return.

To all the Sandras and Keanus out there, thank you!

"Don't forget to wag your tail!"

www.ingramcontent.com/pod-product-compliance
Lightning Source LLC
LaVergne TN
LVHW041545060526
838200LV00037B/1152